Heinemann
LIBRARY

Chicago, Illinois

Behind the News | **INTERNET FREEDOM:** Where Is the Limit **?**

J A N E
BINGHAM

Designed by David Poole and Kamae Design
Printed and bound in China by South China
Printing Company

11 10 09 08 07
10 9 8 7 6 5 4 3 2 1

**Library of Congress Cataloging-in-Publication
Data**
Bingham, Jane.
  Internet freedom: where is the limit? / Jane
Bingham.
      p. cm. -- (Behind the news)
  Includes bibliographical references and index.
  ISBN 1-4034-8833-9 (lib. bdg.)
  1-4034-9354-5 (pbk.)
  1. Internet--Social aspects. 2. Internet--
Government policy. 3.
Piracy (Copyright) 4. Internet fraud. 5. Spam
(Electronic mail) I.
Title. II. Series: Behind the news (Chicago, Ill.)
  HM851.B55 2006
  384.3--dc22

                              2006017504

The paper used to print this book comes from
sustainable resources.

Disclaimer
All the Internet addresses (URLs) given in this
book were valid at the time of going to press.
However, due to the dynamic nature of the
Internet, some addresses may have changed, or
sites may have ceased to exist since publication.
While the author and publishers regret any
inconvenience this may cause readers, no
responsibility for any such changes can be
accepted by either the author or the publishers.

Acknowledgments
The publishers would like to thank the following
for permission to reproduce photographs:
Alamy pp. 30 (Bill Bachmann), 39; AP pp. 45
(Empics), 37 (Empics); Corbis pp. 6 (Simon Taplin),
7 (Justin Guariglia), 10 (Neal Preston), 11 (Gail
Albert Halaban), 22 (Steve Prezant), 26 (Reuters),
27 (Wally McNamee), 28 (Reuters/Stephen Hird),
29 (Reuters), 41 (Zefa/Thomas Brummett/Photox),
42 (Christie & Cole), 44; Empics pp. 16 (ABACA),
40 (DPA); Getty Images pp. 21 (PhotoDisc),
23 (National Geographic), 24 (PhotoDisc), 31,
33 (Ionica), 49 (Photographers Choice); photo
courtesy Teenangels p. 35; RayNgPhoto.com p.
47 (RayNgPhoto.com); Redferns pp. 8 (Martin
Philbey), 9 (George Chin), 13 (Tabitha Fireman);
Rex Features pp. 4 (Brian Rasic), 32 (Phanie); The
Kobal Collection p. 14 (Dreamworks); Topfoto
pp. 19 (AP), 37 (Imageworks).

Cover photograph of an eye reproduced with
permission of Science Photo Library.

The author and Publishers gratefully acknowledge
the publications from which the longer written
sources in the book are drawn. In some cases
the wording or sentence structure has been
simplified to make the material appropriate for
a school readership:

Guy Barnett in *The Age* p.27; *Allentown Morning
Call* p.44; BBC Information Service pp. 11, 29, 36,
38, 46; the *Boston Globe* p.15; *Family Voice* p.25;
the *Independent* p.43; *InfoWorld* magazine p.41;
IT Vibe (www.itvibe.com) p.38; *New York Times*
p.33; Newsbytes News Network (www.technews.
com) p.37; *PC World Magazine* p.30; *Pittsburgh
Tribune-Review* p.26; *San Francisco Chronicle*
p.25; *USA Today* pp. 23, 43; *Women's eNews*
(www.womensenews.org) p.23.

Every effort has been made to contact copyright
holders of any material reproduced in this book.
Any omissions will be rectified in subsequent
printings if notice is given to the publishers.

CONTENTS

Any words appearing in the text in bold, **like this**, are explained in the Glossary.

INTERNET FREEDOM

WHERE IS THE LIMIT?

In the summer of 2000, a fight hit the headlines. It involved the pop superstar Madonna and the Internet **file-sharing** company Napster.

An article in the *Register* (an online news magazine commenting on the information technology industry) had the headline "Madonna Single Leaked via Napster." The report claimed: "Madonna, her manager and record label, Warner, are all said to be fuming, and threats against sites found offering the **download** were flying around yesterday."

What's the story?

Months before the release of Madonna's new album, *Music*, a version of the album's title song was somehow "leaked" onto the Internet. The leaked music file became available on the Napster system and people used the **peer-to-peer (P2P)** file-sharing system to download it onto their computers. This meant that thousands of Madonna fans were listening to her song before it was released. All these fans had avoided paying for the song in music stores. They were also hearing a version that the star had never intended to be released.

Reporting the fight

The Madonna music "leak" was widely reported in the press. Some reports voiced the views of the musicians and their recording companies. They emphasized the musicians' outrage at the "stealing" of original material.

Other articles took a different view. The international **news agency** Newscom reported the problem, but simply said that Madonna was "not amused." The Newscom report listed other stars who had accused Napster of damaging their sales. It also included the case of the rap star Eminem, whose sales did not seem to be damaged by file sharing. The Newscom article explained that Eminem had launched an attack on Napster after his newly released album was shared through the service. The article pointed out that "the unauthorized version didn't prevent Eminem from jumping to the top of the U.S. pop charts."

What's behind the news?

The Madonna story was more than just a superstar drama. It reflected some significant changes in the music industry. Behind the news story were some very important questions. Who really owns the music—is it the musician, the recording company, or the fans? Is file sharing a perfectly acceptable way of listening to music, or is it **piracy**—and therefore a form of stealing? Just how much freedom should people have on the Internet? Should people be allowed to do what they like on the Internet, or should there be laws to stop activities such as piracy?

Madonna's song "Music" was leaked onto the Internet months before it was due to be released. Was this a crime, or was it useful publicity for her new album?

MAKING THE NEWS

The press

The news is brought to us via a wide range of **media**. Newspapers, magazines, TV, radio, and the Internet all carry reports and comment on what is happening around the world. Reporters and journalists working in the media are often known by the general name of "the press."

How does the press work?

There are several different kinds of journalist. Some news reporters provide on-the-spot accounts of a news event. Their reports are usually short and factual.

Other journalists investigate the news. Their reports are usually longer and deal with a topic in detail. These reports or articles are often known as **features**.

Investigative journalists do lots of research to try to discover the facts behind a news story. They interview experts on each side and try to cover all the arguments. These journalists usually produce **objective** articles that present several viewpoints.

Sometimes journalists choose to write a feature article that highlights one point of view. These articles may contain a long interview with one or two individuals, quoting their opinions on a subject. A journalist may also choose to express his or her own personal views on a subject. Articles that express a personal viewpoint are generally known as opinion pieces, or **editorials**.

News can reach us through a range of different media. Do journalists working for the Internet have a different bias from reporters in other media?

All journalists rely on the reports of news agencies. The job of these international news agencies is to provide the bare facts of a story. News agency reports aim to be completely accurate and objective. They try to present news without any **slant** or **bias**.

Can you trust journalists?

Very few journalists report facts that they know to be untrue. However, it is possible to present the news in different ways. One of the factors that can affect the way a news story is told is the bias of the paper, magazine, or news service for which a journalist works.

Newspapers, magazines, and other news services often have a political bias. They may be **right wing** and represent a **conservative** point of view, or they may be **left wing** and take a more **liberal** approach. These viewpoints alter the way journalists present their story. The political bias of their paper can affect the choice of facts that journalists choose to emphasize and the sort of people they quote in their articles.

The politics of the country in which an article is being written also has a major impact on the way journalists present the news. In some countries journalists are banned from expressing any views other than the ones held by the government.

WHAT'S THE REAL STORY?

If you look at several articles on the same news story, you will often see that they do not present the story in the same way. In order to understand the "real story" you have to think about the journalists' bias and consider the message that they are trying to put across. Are they including all the facts? Why have they chosen to interview the people they quote? Are they only putting forward some of the arguments? Often, the best way to see the "real story" is to compare several versions of the same story.

STOP THE PIRATES!

In 2000 Metallica (above) took Napster to court for "stealing" their songs. Journalists disagreed on whether the band was right to take legal action.

Taken to court

In April 2000 the heavy-metal band Metallica decided to take legal action against Napster. They **sued** the file-sharing service for "stealing" their music. The band's lawyers stated that Napster was breaking **copyright law** (see page 11) and so it deserved to face strong penalties.

Metallica claimed that when fans downloaded the band's music from the Internet, they did not go on to buy the songs from stores. This meant that Metallica lost income from the sales of their music. The band used their lawyers to trace thousands of file sharers with "stolen" Metallica songs on their computers. They demanded that all these people should be banned from using the Napster service.

PRESS REACTION

The press reacted to the Metallica/Napster case in different ways:

Some reports praised the musicians for standing up to Napster. A CNN news report entitled "Rock Star Applauds Restraints on Napster" quoted musician Ted Nugent in support of Metallica. Nugent said that people should not be able to download music "for free." He said that advances in computer technology should not be used to rob artists of their money from royalties.

Other articles pointed out that Napster had advantages as well as disadvantages for musicians. Some reporters quoted the example of the band Radiohead, which had benefited from Napster. Before Radiohead released their album *Kid-A*, they allowed some tracks to be shared on Napster. *Kid-A* was an experimental album that was not expected to sell very well. Thanks to the interest caused on the Internet, however, when it was released it was a huge hit.

A feature article on the Internet news service CNET took an unusual view of the Metallica/Napster case. It quoted a business expert who said that Metallica had taken the wrong approach. He claimed that the band should have seen the Napster service as a business opportunity: "If I were Metallica, I would have sent an email to the 300,000 downloaders and offered [to sell] them Metallica CDs, shirts and concert tickets."

Some media reports on the Metallica/Napster case quoted the example of Radiohead (above). They claimed that the Internet boosted the band's success.

What are royalties?

Each time someone buys an album or a single, a small proportion of that sale goes to the artist or band who made the song. This money is called a royalty payment. Musicians earn most of their income from royalties. If people download music from the Internet without paying for it, the musicians receive no royalties.

Tricky questions

The reports in the press raised some difficult questions. Napster's system was clearly harming musicians by depriving them of royalties. At the same time, however, it was also creating new opportunities for their music to be heard. What, then, should be done about file sharing?

This was a complicated issue, but the battle between the musicians and Napster was only part of the problem. The major record companies, such as Warner, Universal, and Sony, were also involved.

The record companies join in

Metallica was not alone in its battle against Napster. The rap musician Dr. Dre also took Napster to court, claiming loss of money. However, the most powerful attacks came from the record companies. From 1999 to 2001 the RIAA (Recording Industry Association of America), which represented all the major U.S. recording companies, brought several **lawsuits** against Napster.

The RIAA accused Napster of stealing their material and breaking copyright laws (see box). They also claimed that Napster was trading illegally. Napster's founder, Shawn Fanning, fought back. He said that Napster was not actually selling any songs. It was simply providing a service through which people could swap copies of songs. The courts were therefore faced with a difficult problem.

When the rapper Dr. Dre brought a case against Napster, some journalists were sympathetic to him. They said that the musicians were simply in the "front line" in a larger battle between the giant record companies and the file sharers.

Comments from the press

Many journalists had mixed feelings about the RIAA/Napster battles. They expressed the belief that the recording companies were also partly to blame for illegal file sharing:

- A feature article in the *Economist* magazine blamed the big music and entertainment companies for being "slow to embrace the Internet . . . Rather than putting their product on file-sharing applications, they are prosecuting free-download users for theft." The reporter urged these companies to figure out "how they can harness the Internet."

- A BBC feature report sympathized with the musicians, but not the big recording companies. "The artists are at the short end of the stick but they should point the finger at the record labels because of their slowness in taking advantage of the digital medium. . . . The demand [for music on the Internet] is producing this piracy."

The young founder of Napster, Shawn Fanning, received a mixed response from the press. Some reporters saw him as a criminal, while others presented him as a campaigner for freedom.

Some reporters asked whether a legal ban on file sharing would actually be a good idea. In a feature article in *Business Week* entitled "Napster's Battle: Congress and the Courts Better Sit This One Out," journalist Alex Salkever argued that the new file-sharing technologies should be left alone until the pluses and minuses of the situation became clearer.

WHAT IS COPYRIGHT?

Copyright is the legal right to publish and sell copies of an artist's, singer's, or writer's work. In the music business, the copyright to a song is usually shared by the musician and his or her recording company. The recording company pays the musician for a share in the copyright, and this gives the company the right to prevent anyone else from selling the songs. If another company is found selling copies of the song, the musician or recording company has the right to sue that company for breaking copyright laws.

A changing situation

In February 2001 a panel of U.S. judges ruled that Napster was breaking the law. The judges stated that "repeated and . . . unauthorized copies of copyrighted works were made to save the expense of purchasing authorized copies." The court ordered Napster to stop trading all copyrighted material. This was the end of Napster as an illegal file-sharing service. (It was later relaunched as a legal file sharer.) However, this was not the end of the battle for the RIAA.

By the time Napster closed down, several new illegal file-sharing systems had been launched. These new systems were different from Napster because they did not have a centralized structure. This made it very difficult to trace the systems' creators. However, the RIAA were determined to stop illegal file sharing, which they saw as a major threat to their business. They decided on a new plan of attack.

We'll get you, John Doe!

In September 2003 the RIAA began to sue thousands of individuals who used illegal file-sharing systems. RIAA lawyers employed computer experts who used **spyware** to identify heavy users of file-sharing services. Under U.S. law, these individuals could not be named, so they were all given the name "John Doe."

Very few John Does have taken their cases to court. Instead, most individuals have settled out of court, agreeing to pay fines of between $3,000 and $7,000. Those who fought the RIAA in court ended up with even larger fines.

Taking a wider view

Most press reports on the John Doe cases took a wide view of the situation. Journalists did not simply report the legal cases. They also looked at what was happening to file sharing at that moment and tried to predict what would happen in the future:

- Many journalists commented that the RIAA appeared to be fighting a losing battle. They observed that illegal file sharing has continued to thrive, despite all the efforts of the RIAA.

- Some journalists also reported on the growth of legal file-sharing systems. These are systems set up by the big music companies so that people can pay a fee to download music legally. In an article dated December 2005, *Digital Music News* announced that the Universal Music Group reported a sharp growth in download sales. The article also commented on the success of the Apple computer company. It noted that Apple had sold more than 300 million songs online.

MONKEYS ON THE NET—A HOPEFUL SIGN?

In October 2005 a newspaper carried a story called "Arctic Monkeys Climbing High—Thanks to the Net." The UK *Guardian* reported that an apparently unknown band had just gone straight to the top of the UK music charts with their first song. The article explained that the Arctic Monkeys' success was due to the Internet. For over a year before they released their first song in stores, the band's songs had been available on file-sharing systems. Several journalists saw the band's success as a hopeful sign for the music industry. They pointed out that the band's success showed that file sharing could boost sales, rather than threaten them.

In 2005 the Arctic Monkeys became the first band to rise to fame thanks to file sharing on the Net. Many journalists have seen the band's success as the start of a new trend in the music industry.

Movie pirates

File sharing is not just about music. It is also possible to download videos, games, and even full-length movies. Movie companies have become very worried about illegal downloading. Now that movies are being produced **digitally**, it is much easier than before to copy a whole movie.

Recently, box office revenues for movie theaters have started to drop, and movie companies suspect that Internet piracy is to blame. The latest *Star Wars* movies were subject to widespread file sharing. By the time *The Phantom Menace* reached movie theaters in Asia, box office receipts were far lower than expected. Internet piracy was blamed for this because so many people had already seen the movie on their own computers.

Some movie companies, such as Time-Warner, have taken the Internet pirates to court. They have sued file-sharing services such as Grokster and Kazaa for loss of earnings. They have also tried to get these services shut down.

Reporting the battle

The media have followed Hollywood's battles with interest. Most articles simply report the latest news from the courts. A few reporters, however, expressed a more biased view. They welcomed the fact that peer-to-peer (P2P) file-sharing services were being put under pressure to close down. In November 2005 a report in the *Hollywood Reporter* had the headline "Hollywood Wins as Grokster Agrees to End P2P Service." It gave a very positive account of Hollywood's legal triumph over Grokster.

AN INDIVIDUAL VIEW

An article in the *Boston Globe* took a more personal angle on the question of downloading movies. In an article headed "The Downloaders Strike Back," Jimmy Guterman described the experience of downloading a pirated copy of a *Star Wars* movie. He admitted that viewing the movie on his computer was disappointing, and he closed up his computer file after less than three minutes. "Watching Jedi joust across a laptop screen is not the way to enjoy something as loud, fast, and blunt as a *Star Wars* film. I could transfer the file to a DVD and view it on a larger television screen, but if I want the real experience of seeing the movie, I have no choice but to see it at a theater. Forget legal arguments or feelings of guilt. Paying to see *Revenge of the Sith* on the big screen is the best way to enjoy this sort of big entertainment—at least until downloaders figure out how to steal entire movie theaters."

Hours after the public release of *Shrek 2*, the movie was available on file-sharing networks. Nobody knows how many viewers watched *Shrek 2* at home instead of paying to see it in the theater.

Freedom of speech

The Internet gives people the chance to express their views on any subject. Anyone can set up a website or **blog** and use it to state their views and opinions. People can also express themselves in online **discussion forums** and **chat rooms**.

These new ways of communicating are all opportunities for freedom of speech. Freedom of speech is a basic **human right** in many countries of the world. In the United States, the right to free speech is defined in the **First Amendment** (see box).

Freedom of speech does not just refer to the spoken word. It also gives people the right to publish their views in books, magazines, and newspapers. However, it is easier to control really extreme views in these media than it is on the Internet. Now, the new question is: Should people have the freedom to say whatever they want to on the Internet?

No more hate speech?

Freedom to express opinions on the Internet can have good and bad results. It means that individuals can speak up against things they believe are wrong. However, it also allows people to express some very extreme views. For example, **racist** groups such as **neo-Nazis** and the **Ku Klux Klan** can go online to spread their views. They can use the Internet for "hate speech" against people of different races or religions.

In 2002 the Council of Europe proposed a law to ban hate speech on the Internet. This issue has still not been resolved.

THE FIRST AMENDMENT

In 1787 the U.S. government created the Constitution. This was a legal document, laying out the rights of all U.S. citizens. The First Amendment was added to the Constitution in 1789. It states that all American people have the right to freedom of speech and freedom of the press:

> "Congress shall make no law respecting an establishment of religion, or prohibiting the free exercise thereof; or abridging the freedom of speech, or of the press; or the right of the people peaceably to assemble, and to petition the government for a redress of grievances."

The Internet gives everyone a chance to express views, but should racist groups, such as the Ku Klux Klan (shown here), be allowed a voice on the Net?

Different reactions

The suggested ban on hate speech resulted in a flood of articles in the press. The response in Europe and the United States was not the same. Many reporters in Europe were sympathetic to the ban, although some pointed out the problems of making it law. A BBC report with the headline "Europe Faces Up to Cyber-Crime Threat" quoted the views of a spokeswoman from a campaign group to stop "cyber-hate." The article ended with her comment on the ban: "This sends out a clear signal that cyber-hate is not OK."

Most of the U.S. media, however, were not impressed with the proposed ban. They saw it as a threat to the right to freedom of speech, as expressed in the First Amendment. A report in *PC World* magazine had the headline "Internet Hate-Speech Ban Called 'Chilling.'" In this article Michelle Madigan quoted the views of several prominent people who were opposed to the suggested ban. The article included the following quote from a lawyer for the Center for Democracy and Technology: "As disturbing as this kind of [hate] speech is, it is protected by the First Amendment. Our vision of the Internet is a free exchange of ideas, but Europe takes a different approach."

Danger for sale?

The Internet gives extreme groups the freedom to communicate their ideas online. It can also give these groups the opportunity to sell items connected with their ideas. For example, neo-Nazi groups have used the Internet to sell Nazi items such as helmets and medals from World War II. Some people think that this is dangerous and wrong. They believe that the sale of items connected with extreme ideas can help to spread and encourage those ideas.

No more Nazis!

By the start of the 21st century, many people in France were worried about a growing neo-Nazi movement in their country. Some people believed that this movement was encouraged by the sale of Nazi items on the Internet. In early 2000 the French government took the Internet giant Yahoo! to court. Their aim was to stop the sale of Nazi items through the Yahoo! site. They also wanted to fine Yahoo!, at a daily rate, for every day that the company allowed the trade in Nazi items to continue. A French court ruled in favor of the French government and ordered Yahoo! to pay a massive fine.

Yahoo! decided to fight back. They took their case to a U.S. court and asked the court to decide whether they had to obey the French court's ruling. Yahoo!'s lawyers claimed that they were a U.S.-based company and that the French government's action went against the spirit of the First Amendment— the right of every citizen to freedom of speech.

The Yahoo! legal battles ran for five years. However, in January 2006 a U.S. court finally decided that the French government's case against Yahoo! was justified. The judges ruled that, in this case, Yahoo! should be subject to the laws of a national government. However, the judges also recognized that "First Amendment issues arising out of international Internet use were new, important, and difficult." They said that lawyers should proceed with caution in this new, untested area of law.

Raising questions

The legal battles of Yahoo! were reported all over the world. Some journalists raised important questions. Did the French ban threaten the right to free speech on the Internet? What kind of materials could be for sale on the Internet? Should a company such as Yahoo! be allowed to have so much power?

In January 2001 *PC World* magazine ran an article with the headline "Yahoo's Nazi Ban Draws Free Speech Concerns." The article raised the question of the "long-term legal and free-speech consequences" of the French ban. Many other U.S. journalists also emphasized the case for freedom of speech.

The French government sees the sale of Nazi items on the Internet as a way of encouraging neo-Nazis (shown here). However, when the government took Yahoo! to court, there were mixed reactions in the press.

A critical voice

Not all members of the press were sympathetic to Yahoo!'s point of view. In January 2006 the *Register* (an online news magazine) reported that Yahoo! had finally lost its lawsuit in the United States. The reporter commented that even though the law case had made Yahoo! "a darling of the free speech campaigners," the company did not always support free speech. He revealed that Yahoo! had recently handed over the details of a Chinese journalist to the Chinese government. As a result of Yahoo!'s action, the journalist—who was a critic of the government—had been imprisoned. The article ended challenging this contradiction: "There's free speech, and there's free speech."

NANNIES ON THE NET

Internet dangers

Hate speech is not the only problem in the Internet. There is also the growing problem of **pornography**.

By the mid-1990s, pornography on the Net had become a massive problem. Many people were concerned that children were able to access websites that contained shocking and distressing material.

Families and schools could buy **filters** for their computers, which blocked out most of the unsuitable material, but computers in public libraries had no such checks. Children often used these public computers, and some people feared that the young people who used them were at risk from exposure to pornography.

Pornography or freedom?

In the United States, conservative groups, such as Concerned Women for America, demanded that the government take action to prevent children's access to unsuitable material on the Internet. They said it was the government's duty to install filters on all public computers. However, **civil liberties** groups were strongly opposed to this kind of government control. They argued that the filters would also block other, harmless information. This action, they claimed, was a form of **censorship**. They said it would **violate** the First Amendment—the freedom of all Americans to publish and access information.

Filter battles

In 1996 and 2000, the U.S. government attempted to pass a law controlling access to pornography on the Internet. Both times the law was overturned in the courts on the grounds that it violated the First Amendment.

Between 2000 and 2003, the U.S. government waged a long legal battle to win the right to install filters on computers in all public libraries. The American Library Association (ALA), with the support of civil liberties groups, opposed the government in the courts. The ALA stated that librarians should not be expected to act as "information censors."

On June 23, 2003, a report on Fox News ran the headline "Justices Uphold Porn Filters in Libraries." The article reported the ruling of a panel of judges, who said, "The blocking technology, intended to keep smut from children, does not violate the First Amendment even though it shuts off some legitimate, informational web sites." Apparently, the long legal battle was over, but what were the real issues behind this story?

A wide range of people, including children, use computers in public libraries. Is it the duty of governments to censor the information available on these computers?

Wider questions

Journalists reported each stage of the "porn filter battle," as it became known. However, their reports soon became much wider than just a simple discussion of a government bill. Journalists became involved in a heated debate about what sort of place the Internet should be. Journalists discussed questions like: Should the Internet be somewhere where people were free to roam,discovering information for themselves? Or should there be **"nannies"** on the Net to protect users from harmful information?

Taking sides

Most of the reports on the porn filter battle presented a balanced view and quoted both sides of the argument, for and against filters. Some journalists, however, chose to highlight the views of different groups in the debate.

Some reports presented the arguments of civil liberties groups, librarians, and other groups who were opposed to the government filters. On the other side of the argument, some articles voiced the views of concerned parents, who were worried about what their children might see on the Net. Some journalists also quoted librarians who disagreed with the official librarians' view and who were in favor of filters in the fight against pornography.

Many journalists have criticized the use of filters on public computers. They emphasize the users' right to access any information they want.

"SMUT AT THE LIBRARY"

A CBS news report with the headline "Smut at the Library" highlighted the views of campaigners for civil liberties. The report expressed the campaigners' fears that "the law would undermine the right to free speech enshrined in the First Amendment." It also quoted the view of a civil liberties lawyer: "Ultimately, the government is trying to dictate what adults can access on the Internet."

"PORN FILTERING WILL BE A NIGHTMARE"

An article in *USA Today* dated June 23, 2003 presented the librarians' point of view. It quoted a library official who predicted that porn filtering would be "an expensive nightmare that would not achieve the government's goal of shielding children from smut." The report went on to explain that filters "can't always distinguish between legitimate sites and porn sites." The reporter also pointed out that "porn site operators have the resources to get around filtering software, leaving libraries with an ongoing struggle to block offensive sites."

"INTERNET FILTERS SCREEN OUT HEALTH INFORMATION"

Some journalists claimed that Internet filters blocked off many valuable medical sites. Their articles claimed that women were prevented from finding information on vital topics such as breast cancer. One article in Women's eNews (an Internet news service directed at women) carried the headline "Internet Filters Screen Out Health Information." Katrina Woznicki stated: "Internet filters designed to block pornographic Web sites also prevent users from accessing health information online up to a quarter of the time. Experts say the filters are bad news for teenagers and low-income people who rely on the Net."

The question of Internet access to medical information has been raised in the press. Can filters on computers prevent women from finding out about breast cancer?

Some journalists express the view that it is up to parents to keep
their children safe on the Internet, but is it really that simple?

Fighting porn

In 2002 the magazine *Family Voice* ran a feature article under the headline "Porn-Free Zone?" In it, journalist Frank York reported: "Citizens are speaking up about online pornography in public libraries—and filters are making them safer for our children."

York began his article with the story of Wendy Adamson, a reference librarian at the Minneapolis Public Library. She described "the horrors that she and her fellow librarians endured after their library installed 50 unfiltered computers. As soon as dozens of pornography addicts discovered they would have unlimited access to free computers they descended on the library . . . Adamson noticed a middle-aged man who regularly brought young boys into the library to see the sites."

York described the campaigns of groups such as Concerned Women for America (CWA) who aim to install filters in all schools and libraries. He quoted Adamson's view that "the great majority of Americans, including teens, want filtering in libraries."

A PERSONAL VIEW

While most newspapers reported the porn filters battle from a **detached** standpoint, a few journalists contributed a more personal view. In an article dated November 13, 2002, *San Francisco Chronicle* reporter David Lazarus gave his own thoughts as a parent on the difficult question "What should concerned parents do about the Net?"

In a long opinion piece, Lazarus considered the arguments on both sides of the debate. He emphasized: "No effort should be spared on the part of law enforcement officials to chase down **pedophiles**, child pornographers, and other predators lurking in the [Internet]." However, he also asked for people to use their own judgment on the issue of pornography on the Net. "Beyond that [the necessary protection of children from pedophiles] I'm not sure what's to be gained from agonizing over a curious child encountering sexually explicit materials online." Pointing to the vast amount of sexual material on TV and videos, he said, "My son will encounter sexually explicit material whether he likes it or not. Just because the Internet makes it easy doesn't make it any more harmful."

Lazarus concluded that the most important role for responsible parents was to be aware of what their children were seeing and talk to them about it: "I can only hope that I'm up to the challenge of discussing what he finds (no matter how troubling) and helping him understand what to make of the strange and stimulating world around us."

Filters don't work!

Even after the U.S. courts had ruled in favor of filters, the arguments did not die down. In the weeks and months that followed, many critical reports appeared in the press describing the problems caused by Internet filtering.

On August 23, 2004, an article appeared in the *Pittsburgh Tribune-Review* with the headline "Porn Filters Expose Flaws." The article began by describing two searches by library users. One was for gasoline prices and the other was for a children's book. Both searches were blocked by the library's filtering system. The article stated: "In the seven weeks they have been mandatory, filters have disrupted hundreds of routine searches in public libraries, according to librarians and patrons. They say the filters have become a counterproductive hassle at best and, at worst, an impediment [block] to the free flow of ideas."

Some reporters emphasized the importance of keeping children safe from Internet predators. This photo accompanied a Canadian news agency article. It shows a young protester expressing her views at the start of an Internet pornography case.

Calls for tighter content restrictions have been made since
the growth in home Internet use during the mid-1990s.

We want filters!

Despite the many criticisms of the filtering system in the U.S. press, there
are still calls in other countries for some kind of government control on
pornography. In December 2005 the Australian newspaper *The Age* ran an
article calling for more to be done to protect young people from Internet
pornography. Under the headline "Keeping Kids from Nasties [predators]
on the Net," Australian Senator Guy Barnett reported that 62 members
of parliament had signed a petition to the Australian prime minister. The
petition called for a ban on access for children to pornographic, violent, and
other inappropriate material via the Internet.

Barnett outlined the case for installing powerful filters on the Internet to
lock children out of pornographic sites. These measures would include
creating blocks on unsuitable material for all computers in the public library
sytem. They would also involve installing filters on materials supplied
through Australian Internet service providers such as Telstra. Senator Barnett
dismissed claims that such a filtering system would be too expensive: "Given
the significance and magnitude of the reform, it could be seen as a small
price to protect our children." He also pointed out: "This reform would be
supported by parents and would have the effect of filtering out pornography
at home and on public sites, with the **onus** being on adult users to apply for
unrestricted access if they wish."

BIG BROTHER IS WATCHING YOU

Censorship

In several countries governments operate a system of strict Internet censorship and control. These countries include China, Myanmar, Cuba, and Tunisia. The governments of these countries allow their people very limited access to the Internet. They also monitor their citizens' activities online.

One of the best-known examples of government censorship takes place in China. Here, the Chinese government has put in place a system of filters known in China as the Golden Shield. To most of the rest of the world, the system is known as the Great Firewall of China.

Research has shown that the Great Firewall of China blocks out websites related to human rights and freedom of speech. People living in China are also denied access to international news services, such as CNN and the BBC.

In addition to operating the Great Firewall, the Chinese government monitors websites, discussion forums, and private email messages. Usually any remarks criticizing the government are rapidly removed from discussion sites. Sometimes people who criticize the government online are arrested.

Internet users in China cannot view this photo of protesters in Tibet. The "Great Firewall of China" prevents people from seeing many websites connected with human rights.

Attacking the firewall

Many articles in the Western press have launched attacks on Chinese Internet control and censorship. In particular, the BBC has been outspoken in its attacks. In an article dated September 3, 2002, BBC reporter Alfred Hermida wrote that the Chinese government "has worked hard to muzzle the web as a forum for free information and discussion." Hermida reported: "China's Internet users face considerable penalties if they are found looking at banned sites. According to human rights **activists**, dozens of people have been arrested for their online activities on **subversion** charges."

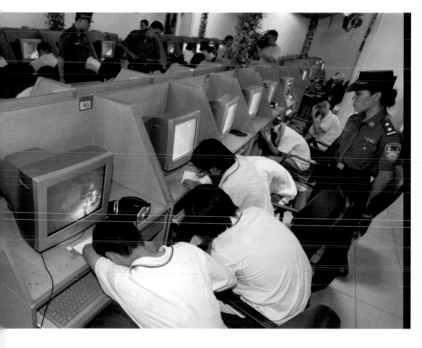

Police patrol Internet cafes in China. Many journalists outside China have condemned practices such as this.

The BBC report also stated that, according to human rights activists, more than 30,000 people were employed to monitor websites, chat rooms, and private email messages. Some Internet cafe managers were said to employ people who patrolled the cafe's computers, checking what material appeared on their screens.

More recently another BBC news report by Richard Taylor (dated January 6, 2006) stated: "China's netizens [net citizens] find themselves surfing in the shadow of the world's most sophisticated censorship machine, which is now more menacing than ever." Quoting an **Amnesty International** spokesman, the report described the fate of at least 64 people "who are imprisoned . . . for peacefully expressing their opinions online." The report ended with examples of the ways that people were managing to avoid the censors and "beat the authorities at their own game."

"China Finds Freedom Behind the Great Firewall"

In May 2004 *PC World* magazine published an article called "China Finds Freedom Behind the Great Firewall." This headline appeared to present a completely opposite view from the BBC reports on China. What, then, was the story behind the headline?

In his article for *PC World*, the business journalist Sumner Lemon explained that he had investigated the Internet situation from the point of view of the Chinese business community. He reported that the Chinese government "demonstrated that it can both censor—and, to some degree, tolerate—the flow of information over the Internet." Lemon quoted Hu Yong, the head of an Internet consultancy in Beijing, who believed that "Western media reports place too much emphasis on Internet censorship." He quoted Hu as saying that the Internet in China is "much more free and open than people imagine."

Lemon admitted that there were "boundaries to this freedom." However, he

also quoted a U.S. researcher, who claimed: "Internet users are often able to access politically sensitive information despite the best efforts of the Chinese censors." Lemon described the growth of some online forums where censorship was not strictly monitored. He explained that these forums reflected the government's recognition that it was good for people "to blow off steam."

Finally, Lemon recognized that the Chinese government was giving its people more freedom on the Internet so that they could make economic progress. He predicted: "The Internet in China will be freed up, not because [the government] desire[s] democracy, but because it makes business sense. For better or worse, it's the money that talks."

China is a country of contradictions. It has all the latest technology, but it is also very traditional. Press reports on Internet use in China often highlight these contrasts.

What's the truth?

Why do reports on the Internet in China differ so much? One answer is that it depends on the journalist's point of view. Take a look at the box on this page and consider the background of the different reporters quoted on the last two pages. Which of the journalists do you think is in a better position to be right? In the end, it is up to the readers to make up their own minds.

DIFFERENT VIEWPOINTS

- Reporters writing for the BBC are aware that the Chinese people have been denied access to BBC news services. In most of their reports, BBC journalists concentrate on the lack of free speech on the Chinese Internet. To illustrate this point, BBC reporters quote human rights activists who describe the ways that the government manages to "muzzle" its people.

- On the other hand, a business correspondent, writing for *PC World*, is eager to report the new business opportunities now growing up in China. This reporter chooses to present a positive view of the Internet in China. Rather than quoting from human rights spokespeople, he presents the views of someone in the business world. He quotes a Chinese Internet consultant who claims that people have far more freedom online than is usually reported.

In 2005 China hosted its fifth Internet Summit, welcoming visitors such as ex-U.S. President Bill Clinton. However, many reporters ask the question: Can China really play a part in the Internet community while it opposes freedom on the Net?

Internet safety

The Internet can feel like a very threatening place, especially if you are young. People can be exposed to threats and abuse from bullies. They can also get into frightening situations with total strangers.

What are the problems of Internet safety, and what does the press have to say about staying safe?

Bullies on the Net

In recent years, the sort of bullying and name-calling that used to take place in school playgrounds has moved on to the Internet. In this new environment, bullying has become even more upsetting and unpleasant. Bullying on the Internet—or cyber-bullying, as it is often known—is a serious and growing problem.

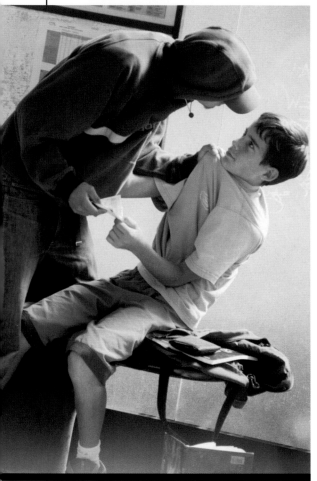

Bullying is always frightening, but bullying on the Internet can feel especially scary because there is no one around to see it.

PRESS REACTION

Bullying on the Internet usually involves sending abusive emails and instant messages to the victim. Cyber-bullies can also create blogs about their victims that are filled with embarrassing images and cruel messages. Other weapons used by cyber-bullies include sending false messages to the victim's friends and enemies. Internet bullies also forward private material to people for whom it was never intended.

Being a victim of cyber-bullying can make you feel very lonely and frightened. Recently, journalists have reported many chilling cases of bullying on the Internet.

Press reactions

At first, journalists were slow to realize the seriousness of the cyber-bullying problem. This was perhaps because online bullying is a problem that usually affects young people, rather than adults. However, journalists gradually became aware of the extent of bullying on the Internet.

An article in the *New York Times*, dated August 26, 2004, carried the headline "Internet Gives Teenage Bullies Weapons to Wound from Afar." It told the story of Amanda Marcuson, who reported some of her classmates for stealing her property. "As soon as Amanda got home," the article explained, "the instant messages started popping up on her computer screen. She was a tattletale and a liar, they said. Shaken, she typed back, 'You stole my stuff!' She was 'stuck-up,' came the instant response in the box on the screen."

The report went on to say: "For many teenagers, online harassment has become a part of everyday life. But schools, which tend to focus on problems that arise on their property, and parents, who tend to assume that their children know better than they do when it comes to computers, have long overlooked it."

The *New York Times* reporter admitted that most schools and parents did not know what steps to take against cyber-bullies. "Many schools, ill-equipped to handle these new situations, are holding assemblies to talk about them and experts in traditional bullying are scrambling to develop strategies to prevent them."

Reporting the problem

Since the early press reports of cyber-bullying, some dramatic cases have become news. There have also been some determined steps to beat the bullies. The media have reported on both these developments.

By 2005 newspapers were carrying an increasing number of reports of cyber-bullying. A CBS news item in March 2005 had the headline "Cyber-Bullying Growing." It reported that a recent U.S. survey found that more than 40 percent of school students claim to have been bullied online. The article included examples of very serious cyber-bullying and concentrated on one case that resulted in the victim committing suicide. It ended with advice to parents to be aware of what was happening on their kids' computers.

Star or victim?

In 2003 a cyber-bullying story hit the headlines all around the world. The parents of a Canadian teenager decided to sue some of their son's classmates for posting a video of him on the Internet. The video showed the teenager pretending to wield a light-saber, "Star Wars" style. The website was viewed by millions of people.

In August 2003 *USA Today* carried an article with the headline "'Star Wars Kid Becomes Unwilling Internet Star." The article reported that the teenager had become world famous, even though he had never given his permission for the video to be shown in public. The reporter explained that there was even a fan club for the "Star Wars Kid," and some fans were campaigning for him to have a part in the next *Star Wars* movie.

The report quoted viewers of the Star Wars Kid website who said that the site was simply harmless fun and not intended to upset the teenager. However, the article also put forward the point of view of the teenager, who was humiliated and upset by all the unwanted publicity.

Fighting for privacy

The *USA Today* report outlined the case of the teenager's parents, who were determined to take the matter to the courts. It stated that there were many who "applaud the lawsuit, and hope it will help set stricter Internet privacy standards."

Finally, the article emphasized the significance of the case for the future of the Internet. It ended with a quote from the director of an Internet safety organization: "I'm hoping we're able to be a society where we do provide people's right to privacy and dignity."

BEATING THE BULLIES

In addition to reporting the problems of online bullying, journalists have also described the growing attempts to keep the Internet safe from bullies. Many articles highlight the work of Internet safety organizations. In particular, reports have featured the work of a group of U.S. teenagers who are determined to fight the cyber-bullies. Known as Teenangels, they are a group of 13- to 18-year-old volunteers who have been specially trained by leading safety experts in all aspects of online safety, privacy, and security. Teenangels run programs in schools to teach responsible and safe surfing to other teenagers, younger children, parents, and teachers.

The media have carried many reports on the Teenangels (an Internet safety group). Here, the group's founder instructs some new recruits.

A safe place to chat?

Many young people enjoy the freedom of Internet chat rooms. They appreciate the chance to talk to others and to exchange views while remaining anonymous. However, chat rooms can be very dangerous places.

In recent years, there have been some shocking cases of pedophiles using chat rooms to "**groom**" young people and gain their trust. Once a pedophile has built up a victim's trust, he or she may arrange a meeting where the victim is **sexually assaulted**. Cases like this have been widely reported in the press.

Press reports

In 2002 the UK press reported the sexual abuse of a 13-year-old girl by Michael Wheeler. According to a BBC report, Wheeler contacted the girl through the Internet when she was 11. He then "groomed" her for two years, buying her presents and taking her to the movies. The article went on to explain that Wheeler targeted his victims by reading their chat room messages and recognizing when someone was vulnerable. Quoting the detective who led the investigation, the article explained: "Wheeler preyed on their vulnerability. He would talk to them about their sexual problems, about problems they had with boyfriends and with their parents. He knew how vulnerable these girls would be."

In 2003 a British court jailed Michael Wheeler for sexually abusing two girls he had met on the Internet. Many reports showed Wheeler's photograph, alongside warnings about the dangers of chat rooms.

Around the time of the Michael Wheeler case, the U.S. press reported the horrific murder of Christina Long by a man who had gotten to know her on the Internet. A report from the Newsbytes News Network stated: "Saul Dos Reis, 25, was charged of using the Internet to entice a minor into sexual activity, a federal charge, and will soon face state murder charges stemming from the strangulation of Christina Long, 13." The report explained: "The girl was slain after agreeing during an Internet chat to meet Dos Reis at a shopping mall." Many of the reports of Christina's death were accompanied by a plea to parents to monitor their children's Internet use more closely. Some journalists also called for law officers to be given more freedom to police the Internet.

Shelley Rilling holds a picture of her niece, Christina Long, outside the court where Christina's murderer was sentenced. The case was widely reported in the media, and journalists called for tougher laws to keep children safe on the Internet.

Police patrols

Once the dangers of chat rooms had become clear, many governments began to consider what they could do to safeguard chat room users. In 2004 the Virtual Global Taskforce (VGT) of police was set up to patrol chat rooms. The VGT is an international alliance of law enforcment agencies, all dedicated to keeping the Internet safe. It includes specially trained officers from the United States, Canada, Australia, and the United Kingdom, as well as many European countries.

The intention of the VGT patrols is for officers to act like policemen "on the beat." The officers visit websites and indicate their presence with an icon or some other device. Then, concerned youngsters can refer to the police if they are worried about any messages they are receiving.

Many people welcomed the VGT patrols as a way to make chat rooms safer—especially for children. However, not everyone was happy with the idea of a police presence on the Internet. The media reported both sides of this debate.

Guardians or spies?

When the Virtual Global Taskforce was launched, many journalists welcomed it as a very positive step in the fight against Internet crime. However, some reporters had concerns:

- In a BBC report with the headline "Can We Really Police Online Chat?" Paula Dear pointed out the impossible task of monitoring the thousands of chat rooms on the Internet. She also quoted child safety experts who were worried that policing measures would lead parents to relax, in the belief that their children were safe. Dear stressed that "the most effective means of tackling online grooming is by educating children and parents."

- Meanwhile, an article on *ITvibe* (an online newsletter for Internet users) voiced some concerns about the new patrols. In a piece entitled "Police to Spy into Online Chat Rooms," Laurence Norah raised the issue that many people feared a "Big Brother" presence on the Internet, checking on their activities. Norah's report quoted a police officer who said, "There is no 'big brother' initiative here. This is about reassurance through visibility." However, Norah's conclusion was undecided: "Exactly how far the authorities are going to intrude into people's private conversations in the name of child safety is yet to be seen."

In 2004 plans were launched for a police task force to monitor Internet chat rooms. Some reporters welcomed these plans, but many expressed the view that "virtual" police patrols would not work.

LISTENING IN

How far should police officers go to prevent pedophile activity on the Internet? Is it enough simply to patrol the chat rooms? Or should they play a more active role in identifying the criminals? In some U.S. states, for example, law enforcement officers pose as teenagers in chat rooms in order to identify pedophiles. An article in the *Arlington Daily Herald* with the headline "Police Hook Pedophile on Web in Five Seconds" described several undercover police operations in Illinois. Toward the end of his article, the reporter raised the question of whether this type of investigation could be seen as "entrapment" (an unfair way of laying a trap for a criminal). This question was, however, immediately followed by a quote from a police officer: "It's simply taking advantage of a situation a predator makes for himself. These people are not being lured into any type of situation."

SPIES AND THIEVES?

By the start of the 21st century, computer spyware had become widely available. Many employers installed spyware on all their company computers, so that they could check up on their employees. Some individuals also bought spyware for their home computers. They used the "spy in the computer" to monitor the Internet activities of their children or even their partners.

Some people think that spyware is a good thing. They see it as a way for company bosses to keep control of their employees by reading their emails and monitoring the sites they visit on the Internet. They also believe that spyware helps to keep children safe. Others see spyware as an invasion of privacy. They question whether computer spying is legal.

What do the journalists say?

The press has gotten involved on both sides of the spyware debate. Some journalists stress the positive side of spying on the Internet. They quote examples of employers and parents who have been reassured by using spyware.

Other reports highlight the worrying side of computer spying. These reports raise the issue of an individual's right to privacy. They often quote legal experts on the question of whether spyware is legal.

In 1999 Scott McNealy, chief executive of Sun Microsystems, dismissed public fears about computer spyware. "You have zero privacy anyway," McNealy commented. "Get over it." This statement caused an outburst of protest in the press.

SPYWARE IS GREAT ...

In May 2003 the magazine *InfoWorld* carried an article on the use of spyware in companies. It claimed: "Being nosy can be good for business. . . . There are many legitimate reasons for an organization to want to know what's happening on its computers. From industrial espionage, to sabotage, and workplace harassment suits, it's not hard to understand the strong financial incentives that may exist for keeping tabs on employees' workstations." Meanwhile, the *Ladies Home Journal* praised spyware for giving parents peace of mind. In an article with the headline "Mother Is Watching," it quoted the example of a mother who used computer spyware to reassure herself that her teenage daughter was safe.

. . . BUT IS IT LEGAL?

In July 2001 a CNN news report by Ann Kellan carried the headline "PC Spies Eye Children, Lovers, Employees." The report described how spyware could be used by employers and parents, but also by jealous lovers to track the behavior of their partners on the Internet. Under the heading "Privacy Concerns," Kellan raised the question of whether such computer snooping was against the law. She quoted a lawyer who insisted that companies should always gain the consent of their employees before they started to monitor their activites on the Internet. However, the law was not so clear when it came to the rights of partners and children.

In March 2005 *USA Today* carried an article by its legal correspondent Eric Sinrod. The article had the headline "All's Not Fair in Love and War When It Comes to Spyware." Sinrod reported on a recent divorce case in which a woman had used computer spyware to obtain records of her husband's emails to another woman. A Florida court found that the wife had broken the law when she spied on her husband. Sinrod commented: "Be careful how you seek to use spyware, as you could land yourself in trouble."

We are being watched! Many reports in the media voice growing fears about the hidden spies in our lives.

Internet shopping is big business, but is it safe?
Many press reports say no.

Is it safe to shop?

Over the Christmas holiday season of 2005, many articles in newspapers, magazines, and on the Internet reported a dramatic rise in online shopping. An article on the Internet news service CNET News had the headline "Online Retailers Report Record Holiday Sales." It reported a 25 percent increase in sales from the same period in 2004.

Press reactions

Many journalists commented on the fact that online shopping was definitely here to stay. Some were very enthusiastic about the new trend. However, other reporters concentrated on the dangers of shopping online. In particular, they warned online shoppers about the criminal practices of hacking and "phishing" (see box). Even the most positive articles usually carried a warning. They urged all customers to be careful to protect themselves from fraud when they were shopping online.

"Forget Santa: Go Online"

On November 26, 2005, the UK newspaper the *Independent* ran a very positive article on a new form of Christmas shopping. The article had the headline "Forget Santa: Go Online for All Your Christmas Bargains." It stated: "Smart shoppers can use the Internet to save a fortune, while avoiding the risk that all the good stuff will have sold out by the time you start looking for gifts."

The article went on to outline the advantages of personal "shopping robots," designed to roam the Internet in search of bargains. However, the report also warned against the dangers of shopping online, since "criminals are increasingly turning to the Internet to relieve consumers of their money and goods."

"Online Grinches Exploit Christmas"

On December 23, 2005, *USA Today* ran a warning piece with the headline "Online Grinches Exploit Christmas Shipping Deadline." It began with a dramatic statement: "Customers have circled Tuesday [December 13] on their calendars—and so have cyberthieves. That's because it's the last day for many consumers to order a gift online and have it delivered before Christmas without paying extra for shipping. It's also the day hackers and fraudsters attack with a vengeance."

The report included some worrying facts. "Hacking and fraud were up 22 percent in the first 10 months this year compared with 2004. . . . And attacks are escalating as a record number of consumers shop online."

WHAT ARE HACKING AND PHISHING?

Hacking is illegally entering a personal computer in order to gain personal financial information. Phishing is using fraudulent emails to trick consumers into revealing their bank account details.

Don't bet on it

The Internet brings the chance to gamble right into people's homes. Is this harmless fun, or is it a way to steal our money? Even worse, is online gambling leading to an epidemic of gambling addiction—especially among young people?

Dangerous or fun?

Recently, several stories about online gambling have appeared in the press. Many have concentrated on the tragic consequences for young addicts who have gotten themselves into serious debt. In these articles, journalists often call for greater government controls on Internet gambling sites.

Not all the articles on online gambling paint such a depressing picture. Journalists working for betting industry magazines, such as *Gambling News*, emphasize the glamor and excitement of online gambling and report on massive wins for "lucky" individuals. Gambling success makes dramatic headlines, and some papers still run stories about big wins.

"INTERNET GAMBLING AT COLLEGES 'VERGING ON CRISIS'"

On December 18, 2005, a report in the *Allentown* [Pennsylvania] *Morning Call* told the sad story of online gambling addict Greg Hogan. Hogan was a highly successful student who was suddenly arrested for robbing a local bank. "Friends, classmates and family were all shocked," the paper reported. However, the article went on to explain that Hogan was "exactly the type of college student who could become overwhelmed by Internet gambling debt and turn to crime to dig himself out of trouble: Intelligent, competitive and otherwise successful."

The Allentown report, which had the headline "Internet Gambling at Colleges 'Verging on Crisis,'" also revealed a larger picture. It quoted the director of a support service for compulsive gamblers: "Gambling on college campuses is epidemic, and Internet gambling is probably the fastest-growing type of campus gambling . . . You give me one hour on any campus and I'll find an active [gambling] game or a kid who can't stay off his computer. It's verging on crisis, and really, we're just getting started."

The story of Greg Hogan, an online gambling addict, was broadcast all over the United States. This is the bank that Hogan was accused of robbing in order to pay off his gambling debts.

"LOCAL TEEN FINDS SUCCESS IN ONLINE GAMBLING"

On December 28, 2005, the CBS broadcasting service reported on a story from the *Philadelphia Magazine*. The article had the headline "Local Teen Finds Success in Online Gambling," and it began: "An 18-year-old high school dropout does not often have a bright future, but one local teenager . . . has left school behind for a lucrative career in online gambling." The magazine reporter explained that Jordan Berkowitz had recently won an online poker championship worth $57,000. However, the reporter was careful to warn others away from gambling.

Online gambling brings the excitement of the casino into your own home. However, some recent reports have pointed out that this can be very dangerous.

Unwanted traffic

Anyone using the Internet has to put up with a vast amount of unwanted material. Some of this material appears as pop-ups (advertisements and messages that suddenly appear in boxes on your screen), but most of it comes through emails.

Emails from companies that do not know you, but are trying to sell you something, are known as **spam**. The owners of the spamming companies, known as spam kings, can make a fortune very fast. In many countries, laws have been introduced to make spamming illegal, and some leading spam kings have been prosecuted. These individuals have had to pay massive fines and agree not to take part in spamming in the future. Meanwhile, computer software companies have created increasingly sophisticated filters to prevent junk emails from reaching our inboxes.

Reporting the "spam war"

Over the past five years, the media have carried many reports on the "spam wars." Reporters have analyzed the impact of anti-spam laws and regulations. They have also considered the effectiveness of spam filters.

Some recent articles report that the situation is improving. A BBC News report, dated December 20, 2005, had the headline "U.S. 'Winning War' on E-mail Spam." It stated: "The number of unsolicited e-mails received in the U.S. appears to be falling thanks to new laws and better technology."

However, not all journalists take such an optimistic view. An article in the computer magazine *PC World* on December 22, 2005, carried the title "Spam Wars Still Rage, Critics Say." It quoted experts saying that inboxes were still bulging and the spamming culprits could not easily be found.

More than 60 percent of today's email traffic is spam.

THE SPAM KING AND THE PRESS

Spam king Scott Richter is a colorful character, and the media have followed his fortunes with interest. When Richter was banned from spamming and was ordered to pay a $50,000 fine, the news was widely reported in the press.

Since then, however, journalists have continued to give Richter plenty of attention. They have reported on his other business ventures, such as his attempt to launch a "Spam King" line of clothing. Have these reports given Richter too much publicity? Have journalists turned him into a celebrity, when he is really just a criminal?

YOU NEED TO DECIDE

The arguments

The question of freedom on the Internet is a complicated subject. People have many different opinions about it. Some see the Internet as an exciting new opportunity. Others believe it is a very dangerous place. They think we need to take action to control Internet freedom.

Think about the following:

- Should Internet piracy be banned?
- Is the Internet helping or harming musicians?
- Is file sharing really just another name for stealing?
- Should people be free to say what they like on the Net?
- Is it ever right for governments to act as net "nannies"?
- What is happening on the Internet in China?
- Should chat rooms be policed, or is this a form of spying?
- Is it safe to shop on the Net?
- Should online betting be banned?
- What can be done to fight spam?

How would you answer the questions above? Can you find additional information in other publications to support your views or to change them?

It seems certain that the Internet will keep hitting the headlines. The press will continue to raise questions about what exactly should be allowed on the Net. Some journalists will call for stricter laws to control the Internet, while others will suggest that governments should keep well away from the Net.

One day you might have to make some decisions of your own about freedom on the Internet. You might have a job in the music or movie industry and need to make some hard choices about the Internet. You might be a journalist, a lawyer, or a politician. You could be involved in policing the Net or in defending its freedoms. How will you use the media to learn about news and events? Will you know how to find out which reports are accurate and objective? Will you hear and respect opposing views?

It will be up to you to look behind the news and find the real story.

One day you may have to make some difficult decisions about Internet freedom. Will you be able to judge whether the media are telling the truth?

1969

A very early version of the Internet is launched in the United States. Known as ARPA (Advanced Research Projects Agency), it is designed to act as a communications network between research, education, and government organizations.

1972

Electronic mail is introduced. The symbol @ is used to distinguish between the sender's name and the network name in the email address.

1982

The word "Internet" is used for the first time.

1984

Domain Name System (DNS) is established, with network addresses identified by extensions such as .com, .org, and .edu.

Writer William Gibson first uses the term "cyberspace."

1989

Tim Berners-Lee of CERN (European Laboratory for Particle Physics) develops a new technique for sharing information on the Internet. He calls it the World Wide Web. The Web permits the user to connect to documents on different sites on the Internet.

1993

The first search engines are introduced.

1994

Mass marketing campaigns are launched via email, introducing the term "spamming" to the Internet vocabulary.

1998

The Google search engine is launched.

1999

College student Shawn Fanning invents Napster, a computer application that allows users to swap music over the Internet. By the end of the year, the RIAA has begun its legal battle against Napster.

"E-commerce" becomes a new addition to Internet vocabulary, as online shopping rapidly spreads.

2000

April   The band Metallica joins the RIAA (Recording Industry Association of America) in suing Napster

May   A French judge orders Yahoo! to stop selling Nazi items online. Yahoo! decides to appeal to the U.S. courts.

June   Madonna's single "Music" is leaked onto Napster.

2001

February   A U.S. court orders Napster to stop trading all copyrighted material.

November The Council of Europe proposes a law to outlaw hate speech on the Internet.

2003

April   Apple Computers launches Apple iTunes Music Store.

June   The U.S. government wins the right to use filters in public libraries.

September The RIAA begins its series of "John Doe" court cases against individual file sharers.

December Spam now accounts for about half of all emails. President George W. Bush signs the Controlling the Assault of Non-Solicited Pornography and Marketing Act of 2003 (CAN-SPAM Act), which is intended to help individuals and businesses control the amount of spam they receive. An international conference of law enforcement agencies decides to set up the Virtual Global Taskforce (VGT) to patrol Internet chat rooms.

2005

July   "Spam King" Scott Richter is banned from spamming and ordered to pay a massive fine.

2005

December The music and movie company Time-Warner wins a court battle against the file-sharing service Grokster.

2006

January   A U.S. court rules that the French legal ruling against Yahoo! is justified.

GLOSSARY

activist someone who campaigns for political or social change

Amnesty International independent international organization that supports human rights

bias emphasis for or against a particular viewpoint. For example, an article can be biased toward a particular political party.

blog (weblog) personal website where users record opinions, links to other sites, and more on a regular basis

censorship practice of examining books, movies, news, and other information and removing content that is considered unacceptable or dangerous

chat room area on the Internet where people can communicate

civil liberties legal rights of citizens to freedom of speech and other freedoms

conservative holding traditional values

copyright law legal right to publish and sell copies of an artist's, singer's, or writer's work

detached not involved in the situation

digital means of recording music, movies, and pictures

discussion forum place on the Internet where people can discuss and exchange ideas or views on a particular issue

download copy data from one computer system to another or to a disk

editorial article, or opinion piece, in which the writer or editor expresses his or her own opinion on an issue

feature article in a newspaper or magazine concerned with a particular topic

file sharing sharing music files or other kinds of files within a network of computers

filter something that blocks certain information

First Amendment part of the Constitution of the United States. It states that all Americans have the right to freedom of speech and freedom of the press.

groom prepare someone online for a sexual relationship

human rights rights that are believed to belong to every person, such as access to food and water

investigative journalist journalist who researches particular news stories to find the facts in more detail. The articles written are often known as features.

Ku Klux Klan extreme right-wing, secret society in the United States, which began after the Civil War (1861–65). Members of the Klan were against African Americans being freed from slavery and carried out violent attacks on many

African Americans. The Klan still exists today, and members usually wear white robes and hoods to disguise themselves.

lawsuit claim or dispute brought to a court for a decision to be made in favor of one side or the other

left wing reforming or progressive political party

liberal holding progressive values

media means of communication, including newspapers, magazines, radio and television programs, and the Internet

nanny person who is specially trained to take care of other people's children

neo-Nazi member of an organization similar to the German Nazi Party, which was led by Adolf Hitler during World War II. Nazis hold extreme racist or nationalist views.

news agency organization that collects news items and distributes them to newspapers and broadcasters

objective representing facts without personal opinions or bias

onus responsibility

pedophile someone who is sexually attracted to children and young teenagers

peer-to-peer (P2P) computer network in which each computer has shared access to files

piracy unauthorized use or copying of another's work. Examples of piracy include illegal downloads of music and movies from the Internet.

pornography images and texts that are sexually explicit

racist person who believes that people are inferior or superior according to their race or the color of their skin

right wing conservative political party that usually does not want to reform society

sexually assault to attack someone with the aim of having sexual relations with a person against their will

slant particular point of view from which something is seen or presented

spam junk emails that try to advertise and sell various products

spyware software that is used to monitor people's activities via the Internet

subversion secret attacks

sue take legal action against a person or organization in order to gain money

violate break, or go against, a rule or agreement

FIND OUT MORE

Books

Clarke, Duncan, and Peter Buckley. *The Rough Guide to the Internet*.
New York: Rough Guides, 2005.

Graham, Ian. *Science at the Edge: Internet Revolution*. Chicago:
Heinemann Library, 2003.

McIntosh, Neil. *Face the Facts: Cyber Crime*. Chicago:
Raintree, 2003.

Rooney, Anne. *The Cutting Edge: Computers*. Chicago: Heinemann Library,
2006.

Useful websites

There are lots of websites on the Internet related to Internet freedom. You
can use a search engine to look up whichever topic interests you. Some
websites that might be useful include:

www.isoc.org/internet/issues/
This page of the Internet Society's website includes links to articles on
different Internet issues, such as censorship, copyright, and spam.

www.i-freedom.org/
The website of the Internet Freedom Association. It includes up-to-date
articles on a range of issues connected with freedom and censorship on the
Internet.

www.learnthenet.com/english/animate/animate.htm
A website with animations showing how the Internet works, including
sections on Internet shopping, newsgroups, and emails.

www.amnesty.ca/china/internetfreedom/
This page on the Amnesty International website provides news and reports
of the latest developments concerning Internet freedom in China. There are
also ideas for how you can help.

www.ala.org/
The homepage of the American Library Association.

www.cybercrime.gov/
Almost anything you could need to know about cyber crime can be found at
this U.S. Department of Justice website.

www.ftc.gov/bcp/conline/pubs/alerts/spywarealrt.htm
Learn how to lower your computer's risk of spyware infections by reading the guide on this web page.

www.cybercrime.gov/rules/kidinternet.htm
This website contains tips on using the Internet safely.

www.rsf.org/article.php3?id_article=10749
More information about the extent of Internet censorship in China.

Activities
Here are some topics to research if you want to find out more about internet freedom:

- Censorship

- Freedom of speech

- The First Amendment of the Constitution

- Spamming

- Hacking

- Internet fraud

- Internet piracy

- The Napster case

- The Great Firewall of China.

INDEX

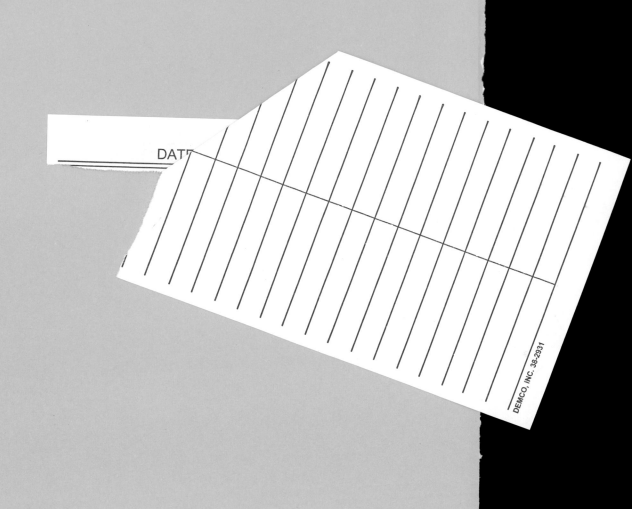

DATE